The
Lighter Side of
Teaching

The
Lighter Side of
Teaching

Aaron Bacall

Skyhorse Publishing

Skyhorse Publishing books may be purchased in bulk at special discounts for sales promotion, corporate gifts, fund-raising, or educational purposes. Special editions can also be created to specifications. For details, contact the Special Sales Department, Skyhorse Publishing, 307 West 36th Street, 11th Floor, New York, NY 10018 or info@skyhorsepublishing.com.

Skyhorse® and Skyhorse Publishing® are registered trademarks of Skyhorse Publishing, Inc.®, a Delaware corporation.

Visit our website at www.skyhorsepublishing.com.

10 9 8 7 6 5 4 3 2 1

Library of Congress Cataloging-in-Publication Data is available on file.

Cover design by Michael Dubowe

Print ISBN: 978-1-62914-723-9
Ebook ISBN: 978-1-63220-028-0

Printed in the United States of America

Introduction

T eaching has always been a part of a spirited debate leading to transformation. Teaching is arguably more than imparting information; however, that wasn't always the case. In 1904 a Nobel Prize was awarded to Pavlov for his discovery of conditioned reflexes. Educators jumped at that idea as a useful model for teaching.

A question was the stimulus and a rote response was elicited and rewarded.

Three years later, Maria Montessori opened her Children's House to inculcate more than rote memorization. She stressed social interaction as a crucial part of education.

In 1909 John Dewey published his seminal theory "How We Think," but the truth is that we still do not know how we think. Perhaps we all think differently and that is not such a bad idea at all. A year later, Lewis Terman wrote "The Measurement of Intelligence." Today we still do not know how to measure intelligence. Perhaps there are various forms of intelligence. How do we measure creativity in a youngster? Is creativity a form of intelligence? Remember that Albert Einstein, a Nobel Prize winner in 1921, didn't fit in properly and dropped out of high school, only to change the world years later. Teaching is a living, changing art. It is not a one-size-fits-all endeavor.

In 1942 I was a mere toddler. That year Anne Frank was forced to leave school and go into hiding. She was not the only one. People yearned for an education, but were denied one based on religion and race. Imagine how she would have welcomed an open and free education. I was starting school when she was scrounging around for food while hiding from government-approved goons. My own parents managed to get a single year of schooling before they had to run and dodge, successfully I might add, the Nazi horror machine. They always remembered and referred to their teacher and the kindness she managed to bring to the classroom despite the political terror and savagery all around her. Education was appreciated. Teachers were given respect. Today, the tide has turned in many schools. Well-intentioned teachers often face student apathy and lack of respect. This complicates the job immensely.

Such students divert precious time and resources from those students who come to class prepared to learn. Students who resist teachers' efforts, who consider schooling an annoying sidebar, and who disrupt the class require intervention from school psychologists, counselors, tutors, mentors and other specialists. Educators reach out to such students and try to bring them into the mainstream, but often efforts fail. These students cannot be abandoned since doing so will sentence them to a life of lost opportunities. This, I believe, is one of the major challenges confronting educators.

In 1994 the U.S. Congress passed the Educate America Act. It was designed to set goals and objectives to be achieved by the year 2000. Most of the stated goals were never achieved. Abraham Lincoln once said that saying a goat has five legs doesn't make it so. That applies to the goals set forth in the Act—i.e., by the year 2000, U.S. students will be first in the world in mathematics and science achievement. Okay, if you say so.

One achievable goal that should have been included is that all teachers will start each school day by reading one funny cartoon and have a good chuckle before they go to class. It's a stress buster, and to that end I offer this cartoon collection.

—Aaron Bacall

About the Author

Aaron Bacall approached cartooning cautiously, stopping at college to pick up a degree in chemistry while drawing cartoons for the college humor magazine, then attending graduate school to pick up degrees in organic chemistry while drawing cartoons as he synthesized glutamate from histidine. All the while he looked for the quirky aspects in all he surveyed. He worked as an antibiotic research chemist and later as a teacher and principal curriculum writer for the New York City Board of Education. He has taught on the high school and college level. He is now a full-time cartoonist and humorous illustrator and is a member of the National Cartoonists Society and is on the Board of Governors of the Cartoonists Association.

His work has appeared in many publications, including *The New Yorker, The Wall Street Journal, Barron's, Saturday Evening Post,* and *Reader's Digest.*

His business cartoons have been displayed at the World Financial Center in New York City, and in 1977 he was awarded first place for the "Best Editorial Cartoon" by United Auto Workers.

To Linda

My Wonderful wife, my best friend, my inspiration
and my life treasure – I love you.

To Darron

An endless source of pleasure and pride – I love you.

To Barbara

A special daughter-in-law and a wonderful mother – I love you.

To Benjamin

A wonderful boy blessed with the dual gifts
of curiosity and imagination – I love you.

To Emily

A wonderful girl with her own unique style – I love you.

To Mom and Dad

I hope you're proud of me. I love you.

The
Lighter Side of
Teaching

"Your heart is slightly bigger than the average human heart, but that's because you're a teacher."

"Wow! I had no idea aspirin came in such large bottles."

"I'm hooked on phonics."

"Good morning Mr. Wilson. I saw your name on the substitute teacher registry. Can you get over to Public School 129 by 9:00 A.M.?"

"I plagiarized it because I thought it bears repeating."

"I made a Valentine's Day card for you. The school has no art supplies so I wrote the color in."

"We're trying to resolve your salary problem or, at the very least, put you on hold for the rest of the day."

**"My teacher and my computer were both
down today."**

"This car was owned by a school teacher who only used it to drive to her stress reduction classes."

"I'd like to run for class president but I don't want to put my family through a background check."

"Do I get part-credit for trying?"

"Read all about it."

"Be careful! This is a tough school. The debating team has a criminal defense attorney to do the talking for them."

**"I don't think my homework is very good.
My dog refused to eat it."**

"I told the dean I couldn't go to detention because I have detention-deficit-disorder, and he bought it!"

"Your report is totally without merit. Add a color cover and punctuate it with clip art then re-submit it."

"Our gymnasium is being repaired so we played sports games on our computers."

"I'm on the school's Academic Olympics team."

"The school computers are six months old. How can I be expected to be competitive in the job market if I'm trained on obsolete equipment?"

"Is it okay if I'm represented by counsel on open-school night?"

PARENT-TEACHER CONFERENCES

"The bad news is your son failed every test I gave this term. The good news is that we know he's not abusing any mind-expanding drugs."

"I start every class with a review of the basics – stay in your seat, don't call out, and don't act out."

"Today in school, we learned how to count to one."

"You mean that's all you ever read, designer labels?"

"I couldn't think of a science fair project so I just re-invented the wheel."

"Can I get a plastic lunch box? This one is metal and it keeps setting off the school's metal detector."

"To fill the budget gap, there will be teacher layoffs. You have the lowest seniority in your school."

"Remember Edward, inside every 'F' student is a 'D' student trying to get out."

"Can you get your mother or father to do your homework for you? You gave me a migraine."

"Do you mind? This is a peanut-free lunch table."

"That's Herman from the math department. He comes in from time to time and gloats. He's on sabbatical."

"Okay, so I failed all the tests and never handed in an assignment. So what's your point?"

"I have to be honest. These college degrees from The Diploma Internet Barn raise a red flag."

"Parents don't appreciate us until winter vacation rolls around and it snows each day."

"His music teacher says he has van Gogh's ear for music."

"I _do_ respect your learning style, but not the part where you crumple paper and throw it around the classroom."

"Having all students read on the level of their choice is politically correct and non-elitist, but I don't think the Principal will accept that as part of our mission statement."

"They can't fire Barney. He has tenure."

"Have you noticed that our wood shop teacher is missing two fingers?"

"The results of your aptitude test cannot identify a particular area that you are well suited for. One thing is for sure, it's not test taking."

"Congratulations on achieving excellent attendance during the last week of summer school."

"I didn't write the report. I printed it directly from the Internet, but I did the stapling and collating myself."

"In general, do the right thing."

"I think we're being educated for failure. We learn math in case the calculator fails. We learn to read in case the TV breaks, and we learn to spell in case the computer's Spell-checker fails."

SUBSTITUTE MUSIC TEACHER PHIL, A NON-MUSICIAN, PERFORMS FOR HIS STUDENTS

"My next selection is something I will now download from the Internet."

"This isn't a good time. I'm in trouble with the Dean for using a cell phone in class. I'll call you back."

"How come the History Channel is so interesting and my history class is so boring?"

"My teacher said the school has tough new standards and I need to improve my vocabulary. What's 'vocabulary'?"

"My teacher says I'm an underachiever, but I think she's an overexpecter."

**"Don't you think this school has way too
many fire drills?"**

"Uh-Oh, teacher burnout!"

THE DANGERS OF UNLICENSED SCIENCE TEACHERS

"The bar magnet has a north and a south pole. The horseshoe magnet has, I guess, and east pole and a west pole."

WHEN TEACHERS' SALARIES ARE TIED TO STUDENT PERFORMANCE

"There are ten questions on this quiz. Each is worth 20 points."

"Must you keep reminding me by wearing that shirt?"

"The classroom is very large and crowded. My seat is in the back and I feel like I'm in a distance learning program."

"It's a guess. I never said it was an educated guess."

"Just because everyone applauded when you dropped your lunch tray in the cafeteria, doesn't mean that you should pursue a career in show business."

"No wonder I'm failing math. I'm just no good with numbers. Even when I dialed the math homework helpline, I got the wrong number. "

"Welcome to Homework Helpline. For help with science, press 2. For help with math, press the square root of nine."

"The students in my contemporary literature class are quoting from deejay Baby Puff Dragon. I have no idea what they're talking about."

"It's a shame how poorly maintained this school is. My graffiti is peeling off along with the paint."

"I went to summer school and helped a few teachers decide not to teach there next summer."

"A focus group of classmates, that I assembled, thinks you can't teach."

"I got tattoos to make a statement, but my teacher said I could do the same thing by joining the debating team."

"Radiology confirms that, like many other teachers of English, you _do_ have a book in you."

"Recess is over now, Edward. If you want a longer recess you'll have to get elected to Congress."

"'How To Do Well In School Without Studying' is over there in the fiction section."

"Remember me, Mr. Sanders? I was a student in your social studies class. You told me I was destined to serve the public."

"A toast to the graduate. You're in a class by yourself."

**"Your anatomy teacher says you're a pain in
the gluteus."**

"I raised my hand and asked if I could leave the room, and here I am."

"My sex education teacher called me a know-it-all."

"Please excuse Harold for not having his homework. His Internet service provider's servers were down and he couldn't connect to his online homework helpline."

**"May I be excused? The pressure
is getting to me."**

"You should think about signing up for a computer course. Every time you finish using the computer, you leave correction fluid all over the monitor."

"It may not be a great report card but it beat the street expectations."